P.L. 89-10 Title II

The "Reason Why" Series

YOUR EARS

Irving and Ruth Adler

Illustrated by Peggy Adler Walsh

The John Day Company — New York

The "Reason Why" Series
by Irving and Ruth Adler

© 1963 by Irving and Ruth Adler

Library of Congress Catalogue Card Number: 63-8553

MANUFACTURED IN THE UNITED STATES OF AMERICA

Seventh Impression

Contents

Your Ears

Your ears are for hearing.

You can hear the voices of people near-by. You can hear your mother calling you to wake up in the morning. You can hear a hungry baby crying for its bottle. You can hear the laughter and shouting of children in the playground. You can hear singing and talking. With the telephone and radio, you can even hear the voices of people far away.

You can hear the voices of animals. You can hear a horse whinny and a donkey bray. You can hear a lamb bleat and a chicken cackle. You can hear a dog bark and a cat purr. You can hear the croak of a bullfrog and the peep of a tree frog.

You can hear other sounds that animals make. You can hear a fly buzzing and a cricket chirping. You can hear the clatter of a horse's hooves.

You can hear the sounds made by ma-

chines that people use. You can hear the wail of a fire siren and the drone of an airplane. You can hear the hum of an electric shaver and the banging of a hammer. You can hear the clicking of a typewriter and the ticking of a clock.

You can hear the sound of music.

You can hear the roar of a waterfall and the clap of thunder.

The sounds you hear help you learn about the world around you. Your ears are like bridges that join you to this world of sound.

In this book you will find out what sound is. You will find out how your ears hear. You will find out how your ears can tell one sound from another and how they can tell where a sound comes from.

You will find out about people who cannot hear. And you will find out how teachers and scientists help these people get messages from the world of sound.

What Is Sound?

You can find out what sound is by making a sound with a stretched rubber band. Stretch a rubber band as tightly as you can. Then pluck it with your finger. You will hear a hum. At the same time, you can see the rubber band move back and forth very fast. If you touch the rubber band while it is moving back and forth, the motion will stop. The hum also will stop. The motion of the rubber band has made the hum.

When something moves back and forth very fast as the rubber band did, we say it *vibrates* (VY-brayts). You can make the prongs of a table fork vibrate by hitting them against a piece of metal. If you hold the fork

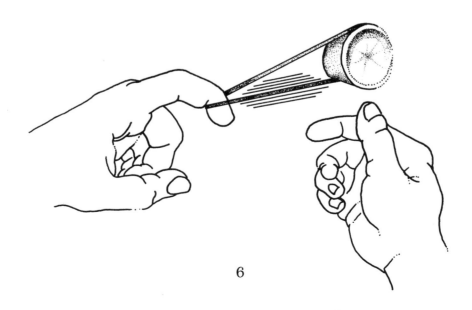

near your ear, you can hear the high, faint sound of the vibrating prongs. If you touch the prongs, they will stop vibrating. The sound will also stop.

All sounds are made by something that vibrates. The sound of a piano is made when a little felt hammer strikes a piano string and makes it vibrate. The sound of a bell is made when the clapper strikes the bell and makes it vibrate. The sound of your voice is made when little muscles in your throat vibrate.

Sounds differ in many ways. One way in which sounds differ is in their *pitch*. A vibrating kitchen fork makes a high-pitched sound. A vibrating drum makes a low-pitched sound. The fork makes a high-pitched sound because its prongs are vibrating very fast. The drum makes a low-pitched sound because its head is vibrating slowly. One vibration back and forth is called a *cycle*. The number of cycles something vibrates in a second is its *frequency*. A high-pitched sound has a high frequency. A low-pitched sound has a low frequency.

You cannot hear a sound unless the sound reaches your ears. The sound vibrations may be carried to your ears by the air around you. If you are swimming, they are carried to your ears by the water. The sound of your own chewing and swallowing is carried to your ears by the bones of your head.

Partners in Hearing

Three parts of your body work together to make you hear the sounds that reach your ears. The ear, the *auditory* (AWE-di-tore-ee) *nerve* and the *brain* work together to make you hear. The ear changes the sound vibrations into electrical signals. The auditory nerve carries the electrical signals to the brain, which puts them together as sounds.

Each ear has an *outer ear*, a *middle ear*, and an *inner ear*.

The outer ear has three parts. What people usually call the "ear" is really the *auricle* (OAR-i-kull). The *audi-*

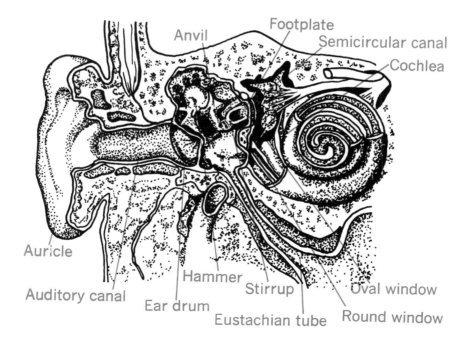

tory canal is a tube that leads from the auricle to the middle ear. It leads to a little window that is covered with skin, like a drum. This little drum, the *eardrum,* separates the outer ear from the middle ear.

The middle ear is filled with air. A chain of three little bones in the middle ear connects the outer ear with the inner ear. The first little bone, the *hammer,* is attached to the eardrum by small muscles. The other end of the hammer is attached to the *anvil* (AN-vill). The anvil, in turn, is attached to the *stirrup* (STIR-up). The end of the stirrup is called the *footplate.* The footplate is attached to a small, oval, skin-covered window. This *oval window* connects the footplate with the bones of the inner ear. A small tube, the *Eustachian* tube (you-STAY-kih-yan), connects the middle ear with the throat.

The main part of the inner ear is the *cochlea* (COCK-lee-a). It looks like a snail shell. It leads from the oval window and has three turns. The last turn ends in another skin-covered window between the cochlea and the middle ear. This is the *round window.*

Three small curved bony tubes are attached to the cochlea. They are the *semicircular canals.* They have nothing to do with hearing. They help you keep from getting dizzy when your body changes its position. They help you keep your balance.

A liquid fills the cochlea and semicircular canals.

9

The Job of the Outer Ear

Most sounds reach your ears through the air around you. The auditory canal is simply a passageway. Sound, in the form of vibrating air, enters the outer end of this passageway. The auditory canal leads the vibrating air to the eardrum, at its inner end. Because the auditory canal is closed at one end, it works like an organ pipe. So the air vibrations are stronger at the eardrum than they are when they first enter the auditory canal. This fact helps explain how we hear faint sounds which come to the outer ear as weak vibrations.

The outer ear of many animals makes weak vibrations stronger in another way. Cats, dogs, horses, cows and many other animals have auricles that are shaped like funnels. They can move their auricles in the direction of

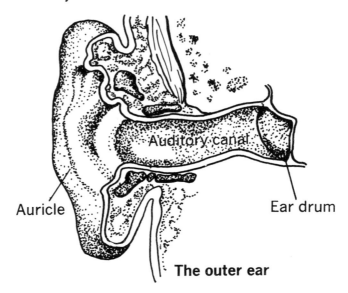

Auricle

Auditory canal

Ear drum

The outer ear

a sound. In this way they can funnel more vibrating air into the auditory canal.

Human beings cannot move their auricles in the direction of a sound. But they can turn their heads in the direction of a sound.

There are many people who can move their auricles a little bit. It doesn't help them hear any better. But it makes us think that, millions of years ago, all human beings may have been able to move their auricles the way animals do.

The auricle of human beings has no use for hearing. Sometimes babies are born without auricles. Then can hear just as well as normal babies can. These babies look odd, because they are different. To make them look and feel like everyone else, doctors have learned how to make artificial auricles out of skin.

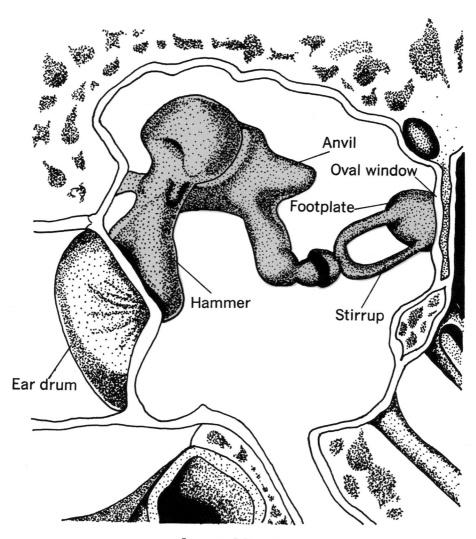

The Middle Ear

The sound vibrations that reach the eardrum are usually weak. These weak vibrations make the eardrum move. But the vibrations of the eardrum are very small. The sound vibrations made by ordinary talking make the eardrum move less than a half of a millionth of an inch.

It is the job of the middle ear to make these sound vibrations stronger. The three little bones of the middle ear do this job very well.

The hammer is attached to the eardrum. When the eardrum vibrates, it pushes the hammer. The hammer, in turn, pushes the anvil. The anvil pushes the stirrup. The footplate of the stirrup pushes against the oval window of the inner ear. Because of the way the three bones are connected, a small push on the hammer is changed into a larger push by the footplate on the oval window. This is one way that the middle ear takes the weak vibrations of the eardrum and turns them into stronger vibrations.

The oval window is much smaller than the eardrum. The bones of the middle ear change the weak push on the larger eardrum into a stronger push on the smaller oval window. This is the second way that the middle ear makes the vibrations that come from the eardrum stronger.

As a result of the work of the middle ear, the push on the oval window is 22 times as big as the push on the eardrum.

The Inner Ear

The cochlea changes pushes by the footplate on the oval window into electrical signals.

The picture below shows what the cochlea looks like if it is unwound. It is easier to see how its parts are connected if we draw it this way. It is easier, also, to understand how it works.

The cochlea is divided into two parts by a wall of cells. The two parts are filled with a liquid. The wall of cells is made up of nerve cells that are connected to the auditory nerve.

A push by the footplate on the oval window is changed into a push on the liquid in the top part of the cochlea.

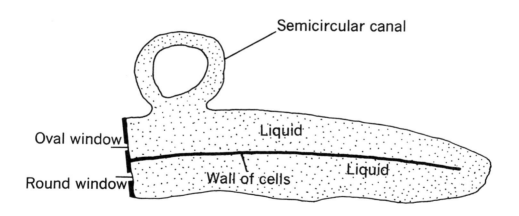

The unwound cochlea

14

This push makes the liquid move a little bit. As the liquid moves, it pushes against the wall of cells between the two parts of the cochlea. The cells change this push into electrical signals. The auditory nerve carries the electrical signals to the brain. The brain puts the signals together as the sounds you hear.

When the liquid in the upper part of the cochlea moves, some of it flows into the lower part of the cochlea. There it pushes against the round window. This makes the round window bulge out into the middle ear. After the footplate stops pushing in on the oval window, the extra liquid in the lower part of the cochlea moves back again to the upper part of the cochlea. Then the round window stops bulging out into the middle ear.

Now you know how all the parts of the ear work together to help you hear. When a sound vibration enters the auditory canal, it makes the eardrum move back and forth. The vibrating eardrum makes the bones of the middle ear vibrate. It makes the footplate of the stirrup vibrate against the oval window. This, in turn, makes the liquid inside the cochlea move back and forth. The vibrating liquid makes the cells that divide the two parts of the cochlea get to work. The cells make electrical signals. The auditory nerve carries the electrical signals to the brain. The brain understands these signals as sounds.

The ear's most important protector is the bony skull in which it is placed. The hard bones of the head keep the parts of the ear from being hurt easily.

The auditory canal protects the ear. It keeps out bits of dirt and other tiny things **that** can damage the eardrum. The auditory canal is lined with little hairs and with cells that make a brown sticky wax. The little hairs help keep bits of dirt from getting into the auditory canal. If bits of dirt do get into the auditory canal, the sticky wax catches them and carries them out again. The little hairs and sticky wax cannot carry out large things that get stuck in the auditory canal. So you must never push anything into it.

The eardrum can be hurt if it gets dry or if its temperature changes very much. The auditory canal keeps the eardrum moist and keeps its temperature the same.

The Eustachian tube also keeps the eardrum from being hurt. When you go up in a fast elevator, you feel a

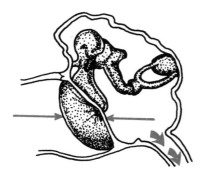

When you swallow, air from the middle ear goes through the Eustachian tube into your throat

16

push against your eardrum. This happens because the push on the eardrum from the outside becomes less than the push on the eardrum from the middle ear. If you swallow or yawn, air can go into your throat from the middle ear through the Eustachian tube. Then the push on both sides of the eardrum is the same.

There are muscles in the middle ear that keep its little bones from being hurt. They protect the little bones from injury by very loud sounds. When the eardrum passes sound vibrations on to the bones of the middle ear, they vibrate in one direction. Loud sounds make the eardrum vibrate very hard. Then the muscles in the middle ear make the little bones vibrate in another direction, too. In this way, the vibration from the loud noise is divided into two parts. Neither vibration is too strong for the little bones. This keeps them from being hurt.

There are two small muscles that protect the inner ear. They help keep it from being hurt by very loud noises. When there is a very loud noise, one muscle makes the eardrum stiffer. The other muscle pulls the stirrup away from the oval window. The two muscles working together keep great vibrations of the eardrum from hurting the inner ear. These muscles do not work very fast. So they do not protect the inner ear from sudden, loud noises like the noises of explosions nearby.

The Frequencies You Hear

Good phonograph records and record players are called *hi-fi*. Hi-fi is short for "high-fidelity." High fidelity means great faithfulness. So a high-fidelity recording of a violin is a faithful recording of the violin. Nearly all the frequencies that the violin can make are recorded on the hi-fi record. Frequencies from 30 cycles to 15,000 cycles per second are recorded on a good hi-fi record.

Although a hi-fi record can produce all these frequencies, not everyone can hear them. The frequencies the ear hears depend on the age of the listener. Most people of twenty can hear from 20 to 20,000 cycles per second. Children can often hear up to 40,000 cycles per second. People forty years old usually cannot hear anything over 10,000 cycles per second. When people pass the age of forty, they hear less and less of the high frequencies. Each year the highest frequency they can hear is 150 cycles lower than the year before. The highest pitch a person of sixty can hear has a frequency of 7,000 cycles per second.

The ear can hear low frequencies, but it cannot hear them well. A low-frequency sound must be loud for the ear to be able to hear it. If this were not so, you would hear all the sounds that are made inside your body. You would hear the sound of your muscles as you walk. You would hear the sound of your head nodding. You would even hear the sound of your blood as it moves through your blood vessels. If you heard all these sounds, they would make so much noise that you would not be able to hear the sounds that come to you from outside.

The frequency your ear hears best is around 3,000 cycles per second.

Some animals can hear sounds that you cannot hear.

Dogs and cats can hear much higher frequencies than you can.

Bats can hear sounds of even higher frequencies. A bat can hear frequencies from 50,000 to 100,000 cycles per second. As it flies, the bat makes a high-frequency sound. The sound bounces back from things that may be in the way as the bat flies around in the dark. When the bat hears its own voice coming back, it knows that there is something in the way. Then the bat can turn so that it will not fly into things.

High-frequency sounds that the human ear cannot hear are called *ultrasonic* (ull-tra-SON-ik) sounds.

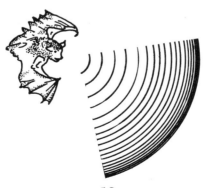

The Loudness of Sounds

A second way in which sounds differ is in their loudness. Two sounds differ in loudness if their vibrations have different amounts of energy.

The loudness of a sound depends on how far away it is. The sound of a gun that is far away sounds faint. The sound of the same gun fired nearby is very loud. By noticing differences in loudness, our ears can help us tell

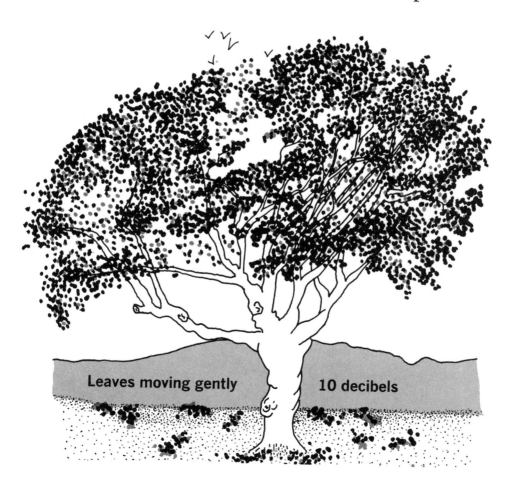

Leaves moving gently   10 decibels

whether a sound is made far away or nearby.

We can measure the loudness of a sound. We measure the loudness by measuring the amount of energy in the sound vibrations that reach the measuring tool. The loudness of sounds is measured in *decibels* (DESS-i-bells). The word "decibel" is named after Alexander Graham Bell, the inventor of the telephone.

On the decibel scale, a sound of zero decibels (db for short) is the softest sound that the human ear can hear. A sound of 10 decibels (10 db) is ten times as strong as a sound of zero decibels. A sound of 20 decibels (20 db) is 100 times as strong as a sound of zero decibels. A sound of 100 decibels (100 db) is ten thousand million times as strong as a sound of zero decibels.

Here are some common sounds measured in decibels:

Leaves moving gently	10 decibels
Street traffic at night	40 decibels
A quiet automobile nearby	50 decibels
Ordinary conversation nearby	60 decibels
Very heavy street traffic	90 decibels
Niagara Falls at its noisiest spot	90 decibels
An airplane engine	100 to 120 decibels

A sound of 130 decibels is not noticed as a sound. It is felt as pain instead. If the sound is very sudden, it can damage the ear.

Hearing with Two Ears

The sounds you hear in one ear are a little different from the sounds you hear in the other ear. So two ears are better than one. Two ears help you find the direction of sound.

One way you can tell the direction of a sound is by the difference in *loudness* between the sounds that reach your two ears. The nearer you are to a sound, the louder it seems. So a sound that is made on your right sounds louder in your right ear than in your left ear because the sound was made nearer to your right ear than to your left ear. Your brain understands this difference in loud-

This sound is nearer to the right ear than to the left ear

This sound reaches the right ear a little later than it reaches the left ear

ness to mean that the sound has come from your right.

Another way you can tell the direction of a sound is by the difference in the *time* when the sound reaches your two ears. A sound that is made on your left will take longer to reach your right ear than your left ear. So the sound reaches your right ear a little later than it reaches your left ear. Your brain understands this difference in time to mean that the sound has come from your left.

If a sound is made in front of your head or in back of your head, you cannot tell the direction of the sound. The sound seems equally loud in both ears. The sound reaches both ears at the same time. So, if you keep your head still, you cannot tell the difference between a sound that is directly in front of you and a sound that is directly behind you. When a sound is made in front of you, you usually turn your head. Then the sound is on one side of your head and you can tell its direction.

Stereo does for hi-fi what your two ears do for you. On a stereo record there are two sound tracks. One sound track is a little different from the other. One track carries the sound your left ear would hear. The other track carries the sound your right ear would hear. Each track feeds a separate loudspeaker. Then the sounds you hear from the loudspeakers seem to come from different parts of the room. This makes sounds from a stereo record seem more real than sounds from an ordinary hi-fi.

The Sounds You Hear

When you are playing or reading an interesting book or watching TV, your mother may call you. She may have to call you many times in a loud voice before you answer. Perhaps she will scold you for not answering her. You may tell her that you didn't ignore her on purpose. You will insist that you simply didn't hear her.

Your mother may not believe you. But what you have told her is perfectly true. This does not mean that your ears suddenly stopped working. It does mean that there

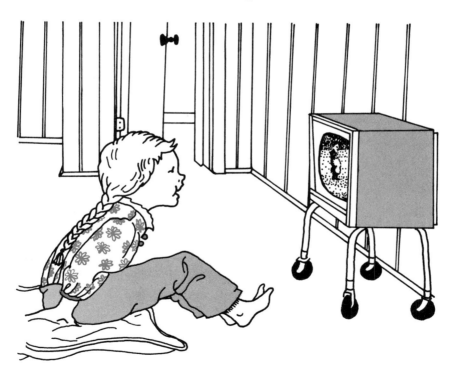

is more to hearing than the three partners in hearing working together.

If you heard all the sounds around you equally well, you would hear a jumble of sounds. Luckily, this doesn't happen. Your ears and brain work together to pick out the sound you listen to from all the sounds that you hear.

The sounds you listen to are sounds that mean something to you. If you hear people speaking a strange language, you hear a lot of meaningless sounds. The sound of their voices gets lost in the other sounds around you. If you hear people speaking a language that you know, then the words sound perfectly clear. Your brain picks out the familiar sound of words that you know.

The sounds you listen to are sounds that interest you. You can easily talk with a friend in a noisy room because your brain picks out the sound of your friend's voice. If his conversation stops being interesting, then your attention wanders. Then you begin to hear other sounds in the room.

It is easier to pay attention to a sound when you know its direction. So two ears make it easier for your brain to pick out the sounds you want to listen to.

Sometimes the sounds you are interested in are drowned out by other sounds. You cannot talk with your friend if there is a siren wailing nearby. The loud noise of the siren drowns out the voice of your friend.

Learning to Speak

Children begin to say words when they are are about a year and a half old. But babies start learning to talk long before they begin to say words than you can understand. Babies learn to speak by copying the sounds of words they hear.

The first sounds a baby makes are crying and grunting sounds. A baby cries when he is hungry. He cries when he is hurt or frightened by a loud noise. When he is a little older he makes laughing sounds and babbling sounds. He moves his hands and feet around as he makes these sounds.

The baby hears the sounds he makes. He hears the voices of his parents as they try to stop his crying. He hears their voices as they play with him and try to make him laugh. He hears their voices as they talk to him while they feed him, bathe him, dress him and carry him. He begins to put the sounds he hears and the motions he sees together. He picks out from the sounds he makes those that are almost like the words his parents say. This is how he copies the words that he hears. The first words he learns to say are words that go with *motions*. So he can say "bye-bye" and "pat-a-cake" when he is about nine months old.

As the baby gets older, he begins to put the words he hears and the *things* he sees together. He learns the names of the things about him. By the time he is a year and a half old he can say the names of many things. Until a baby is about two years old, his talk is made up mostly of these name words. When he wants water, he will say "Water." When he wants to go outside he will say "Out."

The baby keeps hearing the voices and speech of the people around him. He keeps learning the meanings of other words. He begins to speak in whole sentences.

It is important for parents to talk to their babies as they take care of them and play with them. It is important for parents to talk clearly and correctly. A baby cannot learn to talk correctly if he hears baby talk.

"Out"

How Ears Are Tested

Younger people and even children sometimes cannot hear sounds of all frequencies. People who cannot hear well find it hard to carry on conversations with other people. Children who cannot hear well cannot learn well. So it is important to find out whether people have trouble hearing. They can find out by taking hearing tests. Ears are tested one at a time. They are tested by specially trained people.

One way of testing hearing is with an *audiometer* (awe-dee-OM-ee-tur). The audiometer can make sounds with frequencies of 128 to 12,000 cycles per second. The audiometer has a volume control that can change the loudness of each frequency it makes. The audiometer has an earphone that is placed over the ear that is being

Testing ears with an audiometer

tested. The earphone carries the sounds made by the audiometer to that ear.

The audiometer operator makes the audiometer produce a sound of a certain frequency. At first the sound is very soft. Then the sound is made louder and louder until it can just be heard by the person whose ear is being tested. The operator keeps a written record of the frequencies the person can hear. He records, also, the loudness in decibles of each frequency when it it just heard. All of these numbers are placed on a chart. The chart is the person's *audiogram* (AWE-dee-owe-gram).

For most people there is a certain loudness when a given frequency is just heard. Their audiograms look about the same. Their audiograms show what is called *normal* hearing.

When a person's hearing is not normal, some frequencies are not heard until they are made louder than they have to be for people with normal hearing. The difference between the loudness first heard by a normal ear and the loudness first heard by a person who does not hear well is called the person's *hearing loss* for a particular frequency. Hearing loss is given in decibels. When a person's hearing loss is at least 100 decibels, for most frequencies, we say he has lost his hearing.

Many schools test the hearing of all their pupils each year with an audiometer.

People Who Cannot Hear

People who cannot hear are *deaf*. Some people are born deaf. Some people become deaf as a result of injuries. Some people become deaf as they grow older. People who are deaf can sometimes be helped to hear again. In order to help them, it is necessary to find out what part of the hearing partnership has broken down.

There are two kinds of deafness. Damage to the parts of the outer ear or middle ear can cause deafness. Then the outer or middle ear may not be able to carry or *conduct* sound vibrations to the inner ear. This kind of deafness is called *conductive* (con-DUCT-iv) deafness. Damage to the cochlea, the auditory nerve or the hearing parts of the brain can cause deafness, also. Then the vibrations that reach the inner ear never reach the brain as electrical signals. This kind of deafness is called *nerve* deafness.

People who have conductive deafness often can be helped to hear again. People who have nerve deafness cannot be helped.

An ear doctor can find out what kind of deafness a person has by using a *tuning fork*. When the prongs of a tuning fork are hit against something hard, they vibrate. The sound of the vibrating tuning fork can be heard easily by a person with normal hearing.

To test for deafness, the doctor holds the vibrating

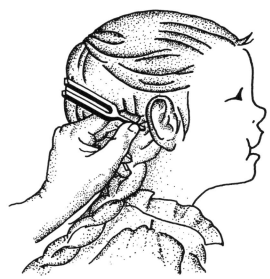

Testing for conductive deafness

tuning fork near the patient's ear. A patient who can hear the sound of the fork clearly is not deaf. If a patient can hardly hear the sound of the fork when it is held near his ear, the doctor then places the stem of the vibrating fork on the bone behind the patient's ear. If the patient can hear the fork when it is held this way, it means that the little bones of the middle ear aren't doing their work. It means that the sound vibrations are being carried to the cochlea by the bones of the head instead. It means that the patient has conductive deafness. If a patient cannot hear any sound, even when the tuning fork is placed on the bone behind his ear, it means that he has nerve deafness.

How the Middle Ear Breaks Down

The Eustachian tube is like a gateway that connects the middle ear with the outside. A gateway can let in things that you do not want. The Eustachian tube sometimes lets unwanted germs into the middle ear. This can happen when a person has a bad cold or sore throat. The harmful germs in the throat may get into the middle ear through the Eustachian tube. When this happens, the bones of the middle ear may be damaged. This is one cause of conductive deafness.

This was the main cause of conductive deafness before 1945. New medicines called *antibiotics* (an-tih-by-OT-iks) keep this from happening now. People with bad ear and throat infections are given these medicines. The antibiotics kill the harmful germs before they can do any damage to the middle ear.

Sometimes the bone of the skull near the middle ear grows in a strange way. Extra bone grows where it doesn't belong. The extra bone may grow into the middle ear. If it grows around the footplate of the stirrup, the stirrup is not free to move. Then the oval window cannot pass vibrations on to the liquid of the cochlea. This is another cause of conductive deafness.

This kind of conductive deafness can be cured by an operation. In the operation, the doctor takes out the stirrup. He also takes out the extra bone that has grown around the footplate. Then the doctor makes a new stirrup out of a small plastic tube. He makes a new cover for the oval window out of a small piece of a blood vessel from the deaf person's arm. After the operation the middle ear can send vibrations to the inner ear again. Then the liquid inside the cochlea is free to move back and forth the way it does in a healthy cochlea. The deaf person can hear again.

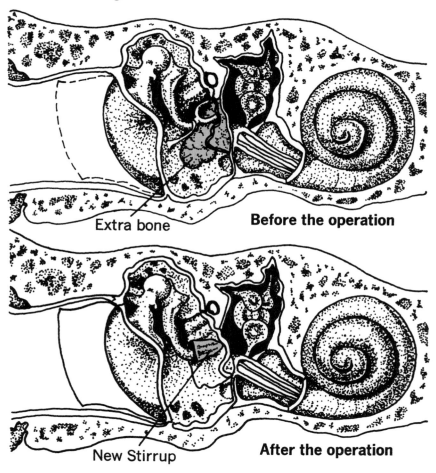

Extra bone

Before the operation

New Stirrup

After the operation

Helping the Deaf to Hear

Many people with conductive deafness can be helped to hear by using a *hearing aid.* A hearing aid increases the loudness of sounds that reach the ear.

Ear trumpets are hearing aids that work like the auricles of animals. The narrow end of the ear trumpet is placed next to the opening of the auditory canal. The wide end of the trumpet funnels more vibrating air into the auditory canal. Ear trumpets are large, so they are not used very much any more.

A *speaking tube* is another kind of hearing aid. The person who is speaking talks into a tube which the deaf person holds next to his ear. Then the sound of the speaker's voice does not spread out in the air around him and

Using an ear trumpet

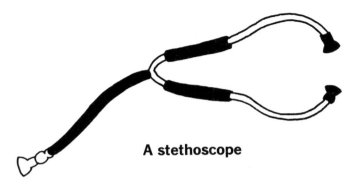

A stethoscope

get weaker. The sound vibrations go right into the tube. More vibrating air is carried to the ear of the deaf person. Speaking tubes are not easy to carry around. So they are not used very much any more. A doctor's *stethoscope* (STETH-a-scope) works in the same way as a speaking tube. It carries the faint sounds that the doctor wants to hear straight to his ear. Then he can hear the sound of a heartbeat. He can hear the sounds made inside the lungs as air is breathed in and out.

The best kind of hearing aid is an *electronic* (ee-lec-TRON-ik) hearing aid. An electronic hearing aid changes sound vibrations into electrical signals. It has a tiny loudspeaker that changes the electrical signals back into sound vibrations the same way a radio does. It has a volume control for making sounds softer or louder. The tiny loudspeaker fits into the opening of the auditory canal. Some modern electronic hearing aids are so small that they can be placed in the frames of eyeglasses. Then they can hardly be noticed.

Many communities have hearing centers. Here a person who has trouble with his hearing is given audiometer tests and other hearing tests to find out if he needs a hearing aid.

The most important sounds for people to hear are the sounds of speech. The frequencies of the sounds of speech are from 250 cycles to 2,048 cycles per second. A person whose hearing loss for these frequencies in his better ear is more than 30 decibels needs a hearing aid.

The hearing center helps the deaf person choose the right kind of hearing aid. The center also helps him learn to use the hearing aid.

A deaf person can learn to "hear" with his eyes. He learns *lip reading*. He pays careful attention to all the

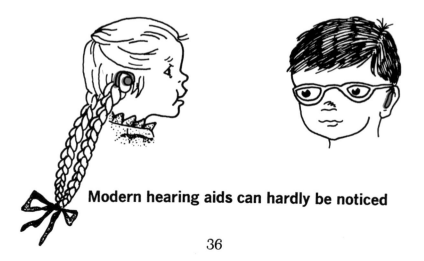

Modern hearing aids can hardly be noticed

face and hand movements of the speaker he is listening to. He learns to know the lip movements that go with each sound. He learns the hand movements that people make when they say certain words or groups of words. These movements that the deaf person *sees* take the place of the sounds that he does not *hear*.

All persons who become deaf should learn lip reading as soon as they notice that they no longer hear words clearly. A hearing aid alone does not make a deaf person's hearing normal. But with the help of a hearing aid and lip reading, a deaf person can understand spoken words.

At the same time that the hearing center helps a deaf person learn to use his hearing aid, it also teaches him lip reading.

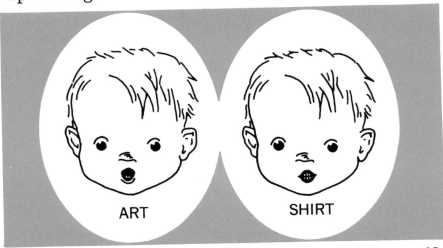

ART   SHIRT

What sound is each boy making? The answer is on page 48

Nerve Deafness

Nerve deafness is worse than conductive deafness. A hearing aid can help many people with conductive deafness. Nothing can be done to bring sound messages to people with nerve deafness.

Nerve deafness can be caused by diseases. Mumps, influenza and diabetes are some of the diseases that may result in damage to the auditory nerve.

Nerve deafness can be caused by sharp blows or falls.

A sudden noise near the ear can cause deafness

A hard blow or fall can damage the cochlea.

Nerve deafness can be caused by certain poisons.

Nerve deafness can be caused by certain medicines. Sometimes a doctor must give his patient a certain medicine to make the patient well. The doctor knows that the medicine may make his patient deaf. He takes this chance so that his patient will not die.

Nerve deafness can be caused by very loud noises. When a sudden loud noise is made near the ear, the two muscles that protect the inner ear do not have time to get to work. So the cochlea may be damaged by the great vibrations made by the loud noise.

Babies are sometimes born with nerve deafness. A baby may be born deaf if its mother has German measles while the baby is still inside its mother's body. A baby may also be born with nerve deafness because it *inherits* its deafness from deaf parents.

When people stop hearing high frequencies as they get older, they have a kind of nerve deafness also. The liquid in the cochlea of an older person does not vibrate as well as it did when the person was young. The weaker vibrations of the liquid do not make all the nerve cells in the cochlea get to work. The nerve cells that have to do with hearing high frequencies stop working. Then the person becomes deaf to high frequencies.

Teaching the Deaf Child to Speak

The child who is born deaf or who becomes deaf when he is still a baby needs a special kind of help. He does not hear the sound of the voices of his parents as they talk to him. He does not hear the sound of his own voice as he laughs and babbles. Soon he stops making sounds. He does not learn to speak.

People used to think that whenever a child did not learn to speak, he could not learn to speak. Then they found out that some children did not learn to speak because they could not hear. They called these deaf children, who did not learn to speak, *deaf-mutes*. As they used the word, *mute* meant *not able to speak*.

Now we know that the deaf child has the same machinery in his throat for making sounds that the normal child has. He has a voice box, with little muscles that can vibrate to make sounds. But he cannot learn to use his voice for speaking because he does not hear the sound of words to copy. So the deaf child is not really mute. He has a voice but he needs special help to be able to use it.

The first person to say that deaf children could be taught was an Italian, named Cardano (Car-DON-o). He believed that deaf children could be taught to read and write. Four hundred years ago he wrote that the deaf child "can hear by reading and speak by writing."

Some people thought that it was wrong to try to teach deaf children. They said that if a child was born deaf, then God meant him to stay that way. It was against God's will, they said, to teach the deaf child to read or write or speak.

There were other people who felt differently. The Abbé de l'Épée (aa-BAY de lay-PAY) of France felt differently. In 1760 he began the first school for the deaf. He taught his pupils to read and write. He taught his pupils to "speak" using finger spelling. To learn finger spelling, the deaf person must learn twenty-six different positions for the fingers of the hand. Each position stands for a letter of the alphabet. Using finger spelling, a deaf person can "speak" only with another person who knows finger spelling.

Cardano

Soon many other schools were begun. In England and in Germany the schools for the deaf taught their pupils to speak with their voices. Now all schools for the deaf teach their pupils to talk.

A deaf child cannot use his ears to help him learn to copy words. So he must use other parts of his body. A deaf child uses his *eyes* to help him learn to speak. With his eyes he can watch all the movements of his teacher as his teacher makes word sounds. He can see the shape of his teacher's lips as his teacher makes each sound. He can see the position of his teacher's tongue as his teacher makes each sound. He can see the movements of his teacher's hands and head as his teacher speaks. A deaf child also uses his *fingers* to help him learn to speak. He can feel the vibrations in his teacher's throat as his teacher makes each sound. He can feel his teacher's breath as his teacher makes each sound. The deaf child copies the movements his teacher makes. He shapes his mouth and

Spelling "cat" by finger spelling

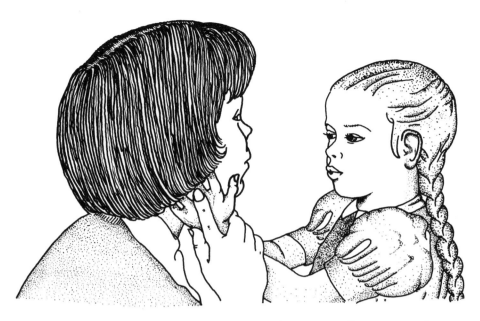

places his tongue as his teacher does. At the same time he makes sounds with his own voice. He feels the vibrations in his own throat and tries to make them the same as his teacher's. He feels his own breath and tries to make it feel like his teacher's. In this way, using the clues he gets through his eyes and fingers, he is able to copy the sounds his teacher makes. In this way the deaf child slowly learns to speak.

Some deaf children can hear a little with the help of a hearing aid. A child who can hear some sound can learn to speak more quickly than a child who can hear no sound at all. So deaf children are often fitted with hearing aids to help them learn to speak.

Alexander Graham Bell: Teacher of the Deaf

We usually think of Alexander Graham Bell as the inventor of the telephone. However, before Alexander Graham Bell became an inventor, he was a teacher of the deaf. His interest in helping the deaf led to his great invention.

Bell's father was a teacher of speech who invented a wonderful way of writing speech in pictures. There was a picture for every sound. The picture showed how the tongue and lips were placed to make each sound. By reading the pictures, a person could learn to speak the sounds of words that the pictures stood for.

Bell thought that his father's speech pictures could be used to teach deaf children to speak. He went to Boston, where he taught picture speech to teachers of deaf children. He used it with his own deaf pupils, too.

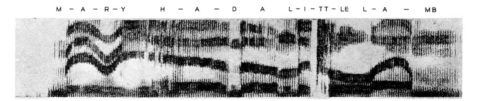

M – A – R – Y   H – A – D   A   L – I – TT – LE   L – A – MB

BELL TELEPHONE LABORATORIES, INCORPORATED

Sounds changed into light patterns on tape

44

When Bell first began to teach the deaf to speak, he didn't think that lip reading helped them very much. He thought that deaf children could learn to speak more easily if they could *see* the sound vibrations that normal people *hear*. So he set about building a machine that could change sound vibrations into pictures that the deaf could see. Bell never did make such a machine. But his experiments gave him the idea that led to the invention of the telephone.

A machine has been made recently that does for the deaf what Bell could not do. The machine changes the vibrations of sounds into patterns of light on a moving tape. Deaf people learn to understand the patterns of light as the sounds that make them. Using this machine, a deaf person can make his own speech clearer. To do this, the deaf person watches two moving tapes that are side by side. One tape has the light patterns that are made by the voice of the deaf person. The deaf person can read the patterns on the first tape as words. He then says these same words. He tries to make the patterns of the words he says just like the patterns on the first tape. When his word patterns are exactly like the word patterns of a normal speaker, the deaf person is saying the word correctly.

This machine can be used as a telephone for deaf people.

Helen Keller: The Story of a Deaf-blind Girl

It is hard for deaf children to learn to speak. It is hard for blind children to learn to read and write. Helen Keller became deaf and blind from a serious sickness when she was a year and a half old. Yet Helen Keller learned to read, write and speak.

Helen was a very bright little girl. She learned how to do many things for herself. She learned how to make herself understood with her own sign language. She did not know any words because she became deaf before she learned to talk.

When she was seven years old, Helen's father took her to see Alexander Graham Bell to help find a teacher for her. A teacher was found for Helen at the school in Boston where Bell had once taught. Annie Sullivan became Helen's teacher.

Miss Sullivan lived with Helen and her family. She slept in the same room with Helen and took care of her. All the time that Miss Sullivan was caring for Helen, she was teaching her.

First Miss Sullivan taught Helen how to "speak," using finger spelling. Then she taught her how to read the raised alphabet of the blind.

When Helen was ten years old, Miss Sullivan began to teach Helen to speak with her own voice.

What happened is like a fairy tale. Helen learned to

speak with her voice. She learned to "hear" the speech of other people. She learned to do this by feeling their lips and throats as they talked. She learned to carry on conversations with people almost the way normal people do.

Helen Keller even went to college. She did not go to a special college for the deaf or blind. She went to Radcliffe College, the college for women at Harvard.

Helen Keller was born in 1880. She is a very old lady now. She has never forgotten her suffering when she was a little girl and lived in a dark world without language. She knows that blindness and deafness are not the only things that make people suffer. She knows that people suffer from sickness and *poverty* (POV-ur-tee) and war. So Helen Keller spends all her time now trying to make the world a brighter, happier and healthier place for all the people who live in it.

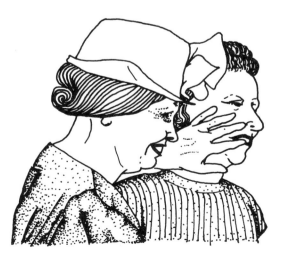

WORD LIST

Audiogram (AWE-dee-owe-gram)—A written record of a person's hearing as measured by an audiometer.

Audiometer (awe-dee-OM-ee-tur)—An electronic machine for testing hearing.

Auricle (OAR-i-kull)—A trumpet-shaped part of the ear that is outside the head.

Cochlea (COCK-lee-a)—The snail-shaped part of the inner ear. It changes sound vibrations to electrical signals.

Conductive deafness (con-DUCT-iv)—The kind of deafness that results from damage to parts of the outer or middle ear.

Cycle—One vibration back and forth.

Decibel (DESS-i-bell)—The unit for measuring the loudness of sounds.

Eustachian tube (you-STAY-kih-yan)—A small tube that connects the middle ear with the throat.

Frequency—The number of cycles something vibrates in a second.

Nerve deafness—The kind of deafness that results from injury to the cochlea or auditory nerve.

Poverty (POV-ur-tee)—The condition of being poor.

Ultrasonic sound (ull-tra-SON-ik)—A high-frequency sound that the ear cannot hear.

Vibrate (VY-brayt)—To move back and forth over and over again.

On page 37, the first boy is saying "ah" and the second boy is saying "sh."